Book Index

Chapter-I

Case Study method of Analysis

- ### Introduction

  - Case studies can be produced by following a formal research method. These case studies are likely to appear in formal research venues, as journals and professional conferences, rather than popular works. The resulting body of 'case study research' has long had a prominent place in many disciplines and professions, ranging from psychology, anthropology, sociology, and political science to education, clinical science, social work, and administrative science.

  - In doing case study research, the "case" being studied may be an individual, organization, event, or action, existing in a specific time and place. For instance, clinical science has produced both well-known case studies of individuals and also case studies of clinical practices. However, when "case" is used in an abstract sense, as in a claim, a proposition, or an argument, such a case can be the subject of many research methods, not just case study research. Case studies may involve both qualitative and quantitative research methods.

- ### Meaning

A **case study** is a report about a person, group, or situation that has been studied. If the case study, for instance, is about a group, it describes the behavior of the group as a whole, not the behavior of each individual in the group.

- ### Definitions

    Case studies are based on an in-depth investigation of a single individual, group or event to explore the causes of underlying principles. Prof. LK Singh

- A case study is a descriptive and exploratory analysis of a person, group or event. Prof. Priyanka Singh

  - ### Features of Case Study Method

- A case study is a research methodology that has commonly used in social sciences.
  A case study is a research strategy and an empirical inquiry that investigates a phenomenon within its real-life context.

- A case study research can be single or multiple case studies, includes quantitative evidence, relies on multiple sources of evidence and benefits from the prior development of theoretical propositions.
- Case studies are analysis of persons, groups, events, decisions, periods, policies, institutions or other systems that are studied holistically by one or more methods.

▪ Types of case Studies

Case studies in research may be mistaken for the case method used in teaching.

In research, three types of case studies are used:

1. Linear,
2. Process-oriented,
3. Grounded.

Under the more generalized category of case study exist several subdivisions, each of which is custom selected for use depending upon the goals and/or objectives of the investigator. These types of case study include the following:

- **Illustrative case studies.** These are primarily descriptive studies. They typically utilize one or two instances of an event to show the existing situation. Illustrative case studies serve primarily to make the unfamiliar familiar and to give readers a common language about the topic in question.
- **Exploratory (or pilot) case studies.** These are condensed case studies performed before implementing a large scale investigation. Their basic function is to help identify questions and select types of measurement prior to the main investigation. The primary pitfall of this type of study is that initial findings may seem convincing enough to be released prematurely as conclusions.
- **Cumulative case studies.** These serve to aggregate information from several sites collected at different times. The idea behind these studies is the collection of past studies will allow for greater generalization without additional cost or time being expended on new, possibly repetitive studies.
- **Critical instance case studies.** These examine one or more sites for either the purpose of examining a situation of unique interest with little to no interest in generalization, or to call into question or challenge a highly generalized or universal assertion. This method is useful for answering cause and effect questions.

- **Merits of Case Study Method :**Following are the advantage of case study Method

1. Intensive Study. Case study method is responsible for intensive study of a unit. It is the investigation and exploration of an event thoroughly and deeply.
2. No Sampling. It studies a social unit in its entire perspectives. It means there is no sampling in case study method.
3. Continuous Analysis. It is valuable in analyzing continuously the life of a social unit to dig out the facts.
4. Hypothesis Formulation. This method is useful for formulation of hypothesis for further study.
5. Comparisons. It compares different type of facts about the study of a unity.
6. Increase in Knowledge. It gives the analytical power of a person to increase knowledge about a social phenomena.
7. Generalization of Data. Case study method provides grounds for generalization of data for illustrating statistical findings.

8. Comprehensive. It is a comprehensive method of data collection in social research.
9. Locate Deviant Cases. The deviant cases are these units which behave against the proposed hypothesis. So, it locate these deviant cases. The tendency is to ignore them but are important for scientific study.
10. Farming Questionnaire or Schedule. Through case study method we can formulate & develop a questionnaire and schedule.

- **Demerits of Case Study Method :Case study method has the following demerits**

1. Limited Representatives. Due to as narrow focuses a case study has limited representatives and generalization is impossible.
2. No Classification. Any classification is not possible due to studying a small unit.
3. Possibility of Errors. Case study method may have the errors of memory and judgment.
4. Subjective Method. It is a subjective method rather than objective.
5. No Easy and Simple. This method is very difficult and no layman can conduct this method.
6. Bias Can Occur. Due to narrow study the discrimination & bias can occurs in the investigation of a social unit.
7. No Fixed Limits. This method is depend on situation and have no fixed limits of investigation of the researcher.
8. Costly and Time Consuming. This method is more costly and time consuming as compare to other methods of data collection.

The cases pertaining to various industries have been solved with the help of SWOT Analysis ,

PESTLE Analysis and porter's Five Forces Analysis .

SWOT Analysis of Google

• Introduction

Google is probably the world's best-known company for pioneering the search engine revolution and providing a means for the internet users of the world to search and find information at the click of a mouse. Further, Google is also known for its work in organizing information in a concise and precise manner that has been a game changer for the internet economy and by extension, the global economy because corporations, individuals, and consumers can search and access information about anything anywhere and anytime. Moreover, Google also goes with the motto of "Do not be Evil" which means that its business practices are geared towards enhancing information and actualizing best practices that would help people find and search information. Though its business practices in China and elsewhere where the company was accused of being complicit with the authoritarian regimes in censoring information were questionable, on balance, the company has done more good than harm in bringing together information and organizing it.

Strengths

▪ Market Leader in Search Engines

Perhaps the biggest strength of Google is that it is the undisputed leader in search engines, which means that it has a domineering and lion's share of the internet searches worldwide. Google has more than 65% of the market share for internet searches and the competitors do not even come close to anywhere that Google does.

▪ Ability to Generate User Traffic

Google is a household brand in the world, its ability to drive internet user traffic is legendary, and this has helped it become one of the most powerful brands in the world. Indeed, Google averages more than 1.2 Billion hits a month in terms of the unique searches that users perform on the site. This gives it an unrivaled and unparalleled edge over its competitors in the market.

- **Revenue from Advertising and Display**

    Its revenue model wherein it garners humungous profits through partnerships with third party sites has held the company in good stead as far as its ability to mop up resources and increase both its top-line as well as bottom-line is concerned. This is another key strength of the company that has helped it scale greater heights.

- **Introduction of Android and Mobile Technologies**

The last of the strengths discussed here relates to its adoption of Android and Mobile technologies, this has resulted in it becoming a direct competitor of Apple as far as these devices, and operating systems are concerned.

Weaknesses

- **Excessive Reliance on Secrecy**

    Google does not reveal its algorithm for searches or even its basic formula as far as internet searches are concerned leading to many experts slamming the company for being opaque and hiding behind the veneer of secrecy. However, in recent years, Google has taken steps to redress this by providing a bare bones version of its unique search engine algorithm.

- **Falling Ad Rates**

    In recent years and especially in 2013, the company has been faced with declining revenues from ads and as a result, the profitability of the company has taken a hit. This is partly due to the ongoing global economic slowdown and partly because of competitors snapping at its heels in a more aggressive manner. Indeed, Apple has already taken steps to garner search engine revenues in its devices and hence, Google must be cognizant of the challenges that lie ahead.

- **Overdependence on Advertising**

Google's business model relies heavily on advertising and the numbers reveal that it gets more than 85% of its revenues from ads alone. This means that any potential dip in revenues would cost the company dearly (literally as well as metaphorically). The point here is that Google has to devise a more robust business model that embraces e-commerce and mobile commerce along with its current business model that is based on ad revenues alone.

- **Lack of Compatibility with next generation devices**

Another weakness for Google is that it is not compatible with many next generation computing platforms including mobile and tablet computers and this remains an area of concern for the company.

Opportunities

- **Android Operating System**

Perhaps the biggest opportunity for Google lies in its pioneering effort in providing the Android OS (Operating System) which has resulted in its becoming a direct competitor to Apple and Samsung.

- **Diversification into non-Ad Business Models**

As discussed earlier, the company has to diversify into non-ad revenues if it has to remain profitable and current indications are that it is adapting itself to this as can be seen from the push towards commercial transactions using its numerous sites like Google Books, Google Maps etc.

- **Google Glasses and Google Play**

The introduction of Google Glasses and Google Play promises to be a game changer for Google and this is a significant opportunity that the company can exploit. Indeed, this very aspect can make the company take the next evolutionary leap into the emerging world of nano-computing.

- **Cloud Computing**

Cloud Computing remains a key opportunity for Google as it is already experienced in providing storage and cloud solutions. Indeed, if not anything, it can move into the enterprise market using the cloud-computing paradigm.

Threats

- **Competition from Facebook**

The advent of Social Media has seriously threatened Google's dominance in the internet world and the company has to pull an ace to deal with the increasing features available on Facebook and Twitter.

- **Mobile Computing**

Another threat to Google is from the emerging area of mobile computing that threatens to pass the company by as newer companies seize the opportunity to ramp up their mobile computing presence.

Chapter-II

SWOT Analysis of Starbucks

Starbucks is a globally recognized coffee and beverages brand that has rapidly made strides into all major markets of the world. The company has a lead over its nearest competitors including Barista and other emerging competitors. Indeed, Starbucks is so well known throughout the western hemisphere that it has become a household name for coffee.

Strengths

- The main strength of Starbucks is its strong financial performance which has resulted in the company occupying the number one spot among coffee and beverage retailers in the world

- The company is valued at more than $4 Billion which is a key strength when compared to its competitors

- The intangible strengths of Starbucks include its top of the mind recall among consumers and by virtue of its brand, which symbolizes excellence, and quality at an affordable rate, the company enjoys a dominant position in the worldwide market for coffee and beverages.

- The company is the largest coffeehouse in the world and because of its size and high volumes; it can afford to price its products in the premium as well as the middle tier range to attract more consumers.

- The company is known for its pioneering people management in an industry where people skills and soft skills make the difference between success and failure. In other words, Starbucks has actualized a positive and welcoming workplace for its employees, which translates into happier associates serving customers in a superior way leading to all round benefits for the company.

Weaknesses

- The company is heavily dependent on its main and key input, which is the coffee beans and hence, is acutely dependent on the price of coffee beans as a determinant of its profitability. This means that Starbucks is overly price sensitive to the fluctuations in the price of coffee beans and hence, must diversify its product range to reduce the risk associated with such dependence.

- The company has come under fire in recent times for its procurement practices with many social and environmental activists pointing to the unethical procurement practices of coffee beans from impoverished third world farmers. Further, the company has also been accused of violating the "Fair Coffee Trade" principles that were put in place a few years ago to tackle this precise problem.

- The company prices its products in the premium to the middle tiers of the market segment which places its products outside the budgets of many working consumers who prefer to frequent McDonald's and other outlets for their coffee instead of Starbucks.

- The company must immediately diversify its product range if it has to compete with full spectrum competitors like McDonald's and Burger King in the breakfast segment which is rapidly growing as a consequence of compressed schedules of consumers who would like to grab a bite and drink something instead of making it at home.

Opportunities

- The company has an opportunity to expand its supplier network and expand the range of suppliers from whom it sources in order to diversify its sources of inputs and not be at the mercy of whimsical suppliers. Further, this would also help the company in becoming less sensitive to the prices of coffee beans and make it resilient against supply chain risks.

- The company has a huge opportunity waiting for it as far as its expansion into the emerging markets is concerned. With a billion consumers likely to join the pool of those who want instant coffee and breakfast in China and India, the company can expand into these countries and other emerging markets, which represents a lucrative opportunity for the taking.

- Starbucks also has the opportunity to expand its product offerings to take on the full spectrum food and beverage retailers like McDonald's and Burger King as the consumer segment which these retailers target is expanding leading to more business opportunities for Starbucks to take advantage of.

- The company can significantly expand its network of retail stores in the United States as part of its push towards greater market share and more consumer segments. This opportunity ties in with the other opportunities described above related to the expansion into newer markets, diversifying into newer consumer segments, and increasing its footprint across the US and globally.

Threats

- The company faces threats from the rising prices of coffee beans and is subject to supply chain risks related to fluctuations in the prices of this key input. Further, the increase in the prices of dairy products impacts the company adversely leading to another threat to its profitability.

- The company is beset with trademark and copyright infringements from lesser-known rivals who wish to piggyback on its success. As with other multinational retailers in the emerging markets, Starbucks has fought litigation against those misusing its brand and famous logo.

- The company faces intense competition from local coffeehouses and specialty stores that give the company a run for its money as far as niche consumer segments are concerned. In other words, the company faces a tough challenge from local stores that are patronized by a loyal clientele, which is not enamored of big brands.

- Starbucks has to expand into emerging markets as a necessity as the developed markets that it has traditionally relied on are saturated and given the fact that the ongoing recession has made the going tough for many retailers, it faces significant threats from this aspect.

- Finally, as mentioned earlier, Starbucks faces significant challenges because of its global supply chain and is subject to disruptions in the supply chain because of any reason related to either global or local conditions.

Chapter-III

SWOT Analysis of Blackberry

Introduction

Blackberry, which was the pioneer in mobile-based technologies with its best selling original Smartphones, has been in the news for all the wrong reasons. First, the company known as Research in Motion (RIM), which made and marketed the Blackberries, missed the emerging Smartphone revolution though it was one of the pioneers of mobile computing. Next, the company was unable to read the market and hence, it lost market share to Apple and Samsung. This resulted in the company nearly going bankrupt and despite changes in leadership; it could never regain its position. In the past month, the company has been in the news again because it rejected a buyout offer and rescinded a sale option and instead, chose to appoint a new CEO along with accepting fresh infusion of capital into the company. This article discusses the changing strategies of Blackberry through a SWOT Analysis, which would provide clues into how the company would position itself in the future. The key theme here is that Blackberry needs to urgently revamp and rejuvenate itself if it has to regain market share and forget about market leadership, it has to ensure that it stays afloat.

Strengths

- Perhaps the biggest strength of Blackberry is that it enjoys top of the mind recall and has a good reputation among corporate users of mobiles because of its proprietary technology that scores over its competitors especially where corporate users are concerned.

- The Blackberry devices can be used with any mobile carriers anywhere in the world and indeed, this is a key strength for the company as it goes along its business with easy mobility and portability.

- One of the main strengths of Blackberry is that its devices are more secure than its competitors and indeed, the security features inherent and embedded in the devices are unmatched by any other mobile maker including Samsung and Apple. This is the reason why Blackberries are so popular with corporate users who use it to link it and integrate it with their VPNs or Virtual Private Networks.

- These strengths have made Blackberry the Smartphone of choice for many governmental agencies in the United States including the FBI, CIA, The White House, and the State Department. Given the fact that Blackberries come with an encrypted military grade security platform makes it the ideal phone of choice for agencies dealing with sensitive information.

Weaknesses

- The key weakness that Blackberry has is that it went on a single-track focus on the corporate users and enhanced its security features as a USP or a Unique Selling Proposition. While this aspect held it in good stead as far as the corporate clients are concerned, once Samsung and Apple came out with Smartphones for the consumers and the everyday usage, Blackberry was unable to keep up with the competition. Indeed, both Samsung and Apple have cornered the market share by enhancing the security features in their Smartphones.

- Given the fact that small business owners using Blackberries now had to install expensive enterprise software, they began to switch to the rivals instead of using Blackberries. Further, the company lost ground as the proprietary operating system used by Samsung and Apple provided more benefits to this customer segment leaving Blackberry out of the race.

- As mentioned earlier, Blackberry was essentially a single pony trick with its obsessive focus on the corporate users. With the large consumer base untouched by it, Samsung and Apple quickly garnered this segment and by providing an easy to use user interface and apps that were simple and effective, these companies soon began to take away even the corporate customers of Blackberry.

Opportunities

- The recent moves by the company are very aggressive as it has rejected a sale offer and a buyout offer as well as accepted fresh infusion of capital from an Angel Investor. By appointing a new CEO and revamping its organizational team and structure, Blackberry has signaled that it is serious and is going all out to reinvent itself.

- The company has a lucrative opportunity as far as leveraging its existing customer base of over 100 Million users is concerned. Given the fact that the company can tap into this customer base for its future products, there is a significant opportunity waiting for the company.

- By integrating the third party apps and features into its phones, the company can mimic the strategies followed by Apple and Samsung and the increase in the business partnerships with third party providers can prove to be a key opportunity for the company as it prepares to take on Samsung and Apple.

Threats

- Though Blackberries were the original Smartphones, both Apple and Samsung beat it to the race to build the Smartphone of the future because they provided the flexibility and ease of use that Blackberries lacked and hence, were able to corner market share and take away its competitors.

- Apart from the threats posed by its competitors, Blackberry has to fight the slack and the gloomy internal environment, which because of the troubles that the company has been through in recent years has resulted in lower employee morale and a general lack of direction. Given the fact that the Smartphone industry thrives on innovation, Blackberry has to rejuvenate itself and reinvent itself apart from rescuing itself from the sagging momentum and motivation of its employees.

Conclusion

the preceding discussion has highlighted the need for Blackberry and its management to take proactive steps to pull the company from the quagmire it finds itself in. The recent strategic moves made by the new leadership are to be seen in the light of the company's drift away from its profit making and market leadership model to a situation where it is no longer in the reckoning. In conclusion, Blackberry and its leadership have their task cut out as they gear themselves to take on the challenges from the Smartphone companies like Apple and Samsung.

Chapter-IV

SWOT Analysis of Amazon

- ## Introduction

Amazon is the world's leading online retailer and its success has spurred other physical, brick, and mortar retailers to have an online presence. It is often referred to as the online equivalent of Wal-Mart because of its reach and global footprint as well as its aggressive pricing strategies. Amazon can leverage on several opportunities in the emerging markets and can ensure that its global supply chain of networked warehouses deliver substantial value for itself and its stakeholders. Further, Amazon has to rethink its business model of operating at close to zero margins and the fact that the company has not returned a decent profit in the last five years gives it much room for improvement.

Strengths

- Being the world's leading online retailer, Amazon derives its strengths primarily from a three-pronged strategic thrust on cost leadership, differentiation, and focus. This strategy has resulted in the company reaping the gains from this course of action and has helped its shareholders derive value from the company.
- Amazon primarily derives its competitive advantage from leveraging IT (Information Technology) and its use of e-Commerce as a scalable and an easy to ramp up platform that ensures that the company is well ahead of its competitors.
- One of the key strengths of Amazon is that it enjoys top of the mind recall from consumers globally and this recognition has helped it enter new markets, which were hitherto out of bounds for many e-Commerce companies.

- Using superior logistics and distribution systems, the company has been able to actualize better customer fulfillment and this has resulted in Amazon deriving competitive advantage over its rivals.

Weaknesses

- In recent years, Amazon as part of its diversification strategy has been "spreading itself too thin" meaning that it has allowed its focus to waver from its core competence of retailing books online and allowed itself to venture into newer focus areas. While this might be a good strategy from the risk diversification perspective, Amazon has to be cognizant of losing its strategic advantage as it moves away from its core competence.
- As Amazon offers free shipping to its customers, it is in the danger of losing its margins and hence, might not be able to optimize on costs because of this strategy.
- Considering the fact that Amazon is an online only retailer, the single-minded focus on online retailing might "come in the way" of its expansion plans particularly in emerging markets.
- One of the biggest weaknesses and something that has been oft commented upon by analysts and industry experts is that Amazon operates in near zero margin business models that have severely dented its profitability and even though the company has high volumes and huge revenues, this has not translated into meaningful profits for the company.

Opportunities

- By rolling out its online payment system, Amazon has the opportunity to scale up considerably considering the fact that concerns over online shopping as far as security and privacy are concerned are among the topmost issues on the minds of consumers. Further, this would improve the company's margins as it lets it reap the advantages of using its own payment gateway.
- Another opportunity, which Amazon can capitalize on, relates to it rolling out more products under its own brand instead of being a forwarding site for third party products.

In other words, it can increase the number of products under its own brand instead of merely selling and stocking products made by its partners.

- Amazon can increase the portfolio of its offerings wherein it stocks more products than the norm currently which places it in a position of strength and comfort as this can translate into higher revenues.

- The fourth opportunity, which Amazon has, is in terms of expanding its global footprint and open more sites in the emerging markets, which would certainly give it an edge in the uber-competitive online retailing market.

Threats

- One of the biggest threats to Amazon's success is the increasing concern over online shopping because of identity theft and hacking which leaves its consumer data exposed. Therefore, Amazon has to move quickly to allay consumer concerns over its site and ensure that online privacy and security are guaranteed.

- Because of its aggressive pricing strategies, the company has had to face lawsuits from publishers and rivals in the retailing industry. The obsessive focus on cost leadership that Amazon follows has become a source of trouble for the company because of the competitors being upset with Amazon taking away the business from them.

- Finally, Amazon faces significant competition from local online retailers who are more agile and nimble when compared to its behemoth type of strategy. This means that the company cannot lose sight of its local market conditions in the pursuit of its global strategy.

Conclusion

Amazon has its task cut out as far as its future strategies are concerned and this SWOT Analysis can provide a guide and a roadmap that the company can implement going forward. The key take away from this SWOT Analysis is that Amazon has to focus on profitability and not volumes alone if it has to be competitive in the future where volumes and market leadership are not alone to add value to its stock.

Chapter-V

SWOT Analysis of IKEA

Introduction

This article analyzes the strategy of the world's leading furniture retailer, IKEA using the SWOT Methodology. The company was founded in 1943 and is known for its simple yet effective approach to retailing with the DIY or the Do It Yourself concept, which ensures that the company keeps costs to a minimum and passes on the value to the customers. The products sold by IKEA are mostly ready to use and flat packed meaning that they can be assembled by the customers themselves. The company has a presence in the online world as well and the total sales from its online and offline businesses are more than a Billion Dollars per year. The key strategic driver of IKEA's success is it's no nonsense approach to retailing that has paid rich dividends for the company and its shareholders (literally and metaphorically).

Strengths

- The biggest strength that IKEA has is its clear vision, which is to add value to its customers irrespective of the market conditions. This has translated into an articulate and well-defined business strategy and an approach to retailing, which is pioneering in its simplicity and deadly in its targeting of competitors and effective in its positioning.

- Another key strength of the company is its clear concept which translates into an array of products that can be assembled by the customers themselves leading to humungous cost reductions which are then passed on to the customers. With its single-minded focus on cost leadership, IKEA has emerged as the world's leading retailer of furniture.

- IKEA measures its strengths using the metrics provided by the KPIs or the Key Performance Indicators that include increased use of renewable materials, smarter use of raw materials, establishing and maintaining long-term relationships with suppliers and leveraging the efficiencies and the synergies from the economies of scale.

Weaknesses

- Given the fact that IKEA operates in multiple countries around the world, it is a high scale and a large size business meaning that it is difficult to control standards across locations. Though the company tries its best to implement uniform quality across its product range and throughout its locations, replicable and scalable control of quality is a key weakness.

- With its obsessive focus on cost leadership, quality sometimes goes for a toss especially in the present context where the costs of many inputs and raw materials has gone up and which has impacted the profitability of the company. The point to be noted here is that it is sometimes difficult to maintain quality in the context of increasing costs and the need to replicate standards across its locations worldwide.

- There are environmental concerns about IKEA's operations and the company faces challenges in communicating and articulating its environmental policies to its customers, shareholders, and other stakeholders.

Opportunities

- With its "green" business model, the company has a huge opportunity waiting in terms of attracting customers who like to buy such products. The rise of the ethical consumer or the process of buying known as "Ethical Chic" which means that customers would ideally like to buy products that are environmentally conscious is an opportunity waiting to be tapped for the company.

- Perhaps the biggest opportunity that the company has is its cost leadership, which means a single-minded focus on cost at the expense of everything else. While this has raised concerns about quality, the customers do not seem to mind as they are getting their money's worth and the addition of value to the customers is another significant opportunity.

- The other opportunity lies in the company's expansion into the emerging markets and the developing world where it has an untapped customer base that can be leveraged for effective profitability. IKEA is already drawing up plans to enter markets like China and

India with a clear strategy of cost leadership, which it hopes, would yield benefits to the company.

Threats

- IKEA's low cost business model has been imitated and copied by its rivals, which means that the company needs to constantly innovate if it has to stay ahead of the competition. For instance, several regional and local companies have caught on to the DIY bandwagon and are also focusing on costs which means that to stay nimble and agile, IKEA has to come up with newer strategies.
- With the advent of the internet and online shopping, DIY as a key driver of strategic success is no longer the sole USP or Unique Selling Proposition of IKEA and with the proliferation of online retailers who can provide even lower costs because they do not have a physical presence means that they are snapping at the heels of IKEA.

Conclusion

IKEA is a well-known global trend and through its innovative business model and its focus on products, processes, and systems, it has managed to stay ahead of the competition in the furniture retailing business. The company can diversify into other products and product lines as it can replicate its business model in other realms as well. To do this would require fresh thinking and a new approach to its strategy that would combine low cost leadership with additional drivers of success like scalability and focus on quality. Finally, the company can enter the emerging markets where its products and its business model are likely to be met with success and the untapped customer base can be leveraged.

Chapter-VI

SWOT Analysis of Nike

- ## Strengths

- The biggest strength of Nike is that it is an extremely competitive organization with its approach of "Just Do It" slogan for its brand epitomizing its attitude towards business. The company was founded on the principle that it would make shoes for anyone who could walk or run and this has been the guiding philosophy behind Nike. Coupled with its iconic "Swoosh" logo and its equally catchy tagline, Nike's strength is that it has emerged as a "Can Do" company.

- Strength of the company is that it has outsourced all aspects of its production to overseas facilities and thereby, does not have any manufacturing outlet of its own. This has helped the company focus on higher value adding activities like design and research and development and at the same time, it has saved the high labor costs that are part of the traditional manufacturing sector.

- Apart from this, the other big strength of Nike is that it is a globally recognized brand that has top of the mind recall among consumers and the youth in particular. Further, the Nike brand is synonymous with quality and resilience as well as endurance and fitness, which makes it the brand of choice for athletes and anyone who wishes to run.

- Finally, Nike stands to benefit from the current disarray among its competitors because of the fragmentation of the market wherein Nike with its USP or Unique Selling Proposition can standalone among them.

- ## Weaknesses

- Nike is almost exclusively driven by its footwear business and therefore, the footwear market contributes to a lion's share of its revenues making it dependent on this segment for its survival. In these recessionary times, it is not a good business practice to be overly dependent on one segment and hence, Nike ought to diversify horizontally as well as vertically and include apparel and other accessories.

- Though we have mentioned the fact that it has outsourced its manufacturing aspects completely as strength, the negative publicity that Nike got because of labor unfriendly conditions in its overseas outlets has badly dented its brand image. Indeed, the name "Sweatshops" is used to mockingly describe the abhorrent conditions in its overseas manufacturing facilities.

- The company does its business through retailers who stock other brands as well. This means that the assiduously cultivated exclusivity is sometimes sacrificed because it has not yet spread its wings to include exclusive retailer outlets as part of its business strategy.

- Nike is perceived by some consumers as being too premium and a luxury brand. While this is necessarily not a bad thing, the current market scenario is such that consumers are migrating to the middle tier of the luxury scale as they are becoming price conscious and quality focused.

- **Opportunities**

- The biggest opportunity for Nike is from the emerging markets of China and India where the Billion Plus new consumers are now aspiring to western lifestyles which means that they would be more receptive to brands like Nike. As the company is associated with premium branding and segmentation, it can be said that capturing the "emerging market newly affluent consumers' prize" could well be a game changer for the company.

- In recent years, Nike has begun to diversify into accessories and other premium products apart its signature footwear segment. This is a step in the right direction and something, which would stand the company in good stead as it attempts to look for revenues beyond its traditional offerings.

- The emphasis on design of higher end footwear seems to be paying off for Nike that is increasingly being seen as a must have product for anyone who walks or runs and as the company was founded on the principle that it would serve anyone with legs, this strategy seems to have hit the right notes.

- Nike has the unique advantage of offering value for money and this can be leveraged to the hilt as the company begins to make inroads into the newer consumer segments, which want quality at an affordable price.

- **Threats**

- The fact that the company has a global supply chain means that it is subject to the vicissitudes of international trade practices including labor strikes in its overseas locations, currency fluctuations that decrease its margins, as well as lack of control over the geopolitical events happening around the world which have the potential to disrupt its global supply chain.

- Nike must improve on its image wherein it is being seen as resorting to exploitative business practices in its overseas outlets. Already, it had to pay a heavy price (monetarily as well as metaphorically) because the emerging generation of consumers are socially and environmentally conscious which means that they would not like to buy a product that is the result of dubious business practices.

- The ongoing recession has taken a heavy toll on Nike with consumers becoming more price conscious and retailers demanding higher margins. The combination of retailing in third party outlets and competing brands cutting prices has made the going tough for Nike.

- Finally, Nike has to ensure that it does not dilute its focus like some of its competitors who are now in the doldrums. For instance, Reebok that promised a lot and was intensely competitive with Nike has seen its fortunes sag and hence, Nike must not go Reebok's way and instead, must define its core competence and implement its strategies accordingly.

Chapter-VII

SWOT Analysis of Microsoft

- **Introduction**

The recent announcement of the change of leadership at the helm of Microsoft has sparked speculation about possible strategic directional changes as well as kindled hopes that the pioneering company and its iconic founder who appeared to be floundering in recent years may well be getting their act together. The ensuing SWOT Analysis places these strategic moves in perspective and appraises the situation, which the company finds itself in at the moment. The succeeding discussion must be viewed in the larger context of the match between the internal dynamics and the external business drivers that affect Microsoft in its quest to regain its market leadership.

Strengths

- The biggest strength of Microsoft is that it has top of the mind brand recall among all the PC (personal computer) users in the world. Indeed, Microsoft and its legendary founder, Bill Gates, are known to anyone who is remotely acquainted with computing. This has enabled the company to forge ahead of its rivals even though as we shall discuss later, in recent years, some of the sheen of the Microsoft brand has been lost.

- The other strength and a key driver of its business and readymade acceptance by the users of its products is that Microsoft's software is easy to use which has won it an increasing base of customers around the world. It can also be said that Microsoft and Bill Gates have spawned what can be called a "Second Industrial Revolution" by making computing available to the masses.

- The company has a worldwide network of distributors and also it indulges in co-branding with hardware makers of computers, which enables it to have strategic depth and a breadth of user base that is unparalleled.

- Microsoft has consistently beat analyst expectations in terms of profitability and revenues though it is appearing to be vulnerable to shifting trends like mobile computing in recent years.

Weaknesses

- The biggest weakness of Microsoft is that its fabled team did not anticipate the emergence of the internet as a phenomenon that would take over the world in addition to reading the market signals about mobile computing. In case of the former (internet), Microsoft was slow to respond and even when it did, it was in a manner that attracted monopolistic charges which in earlier years were the mainstay of the company.
- As for mobile computing, Microsoft completely missed this wave and indeed, the success of the other computing revolutionary, Late Steve Jobs and his Apple Company appeared to blindside Microsoft and Bill Gates so much that it has even now failed to come up with a compelling Smartphone device or operating system.
- The third weakness relates to the ubiquitous security flaws in its software, which is apparent to any windows user, and chances are that you would have probably encountered the familiar crashes of Windows no matter which version you use.

Opportunities

- Though Microsoft failed to read the emergence of the internet and was completely taken aback by the mobile wave, a ray of hope that is still visible to the company is in the cloud-computing paradigm, which the company is betting big to take on the competition and regain its leadership position.
- Indeed, the recent appointment of the Indian born Satya Nadella as the CEO is in line with its aggressive push towards cloud computing as the game changer for the company and since Nadella is thought to be a cloud-computing wizard, it is understood that Microsoft is banking on him for it to ride the next wave.

- The company has a huge cash hoard which means that if it cannot grow organically (through normal growth) it can still grow inorganically (through acquisitions) of smaller companies that have good business prospects.
- This is the manner in which Bill Gates made amends for misreading the internet and bought out Hotmail created by another Indian, Sameer Bhatia that did give Microsoft some edge for a few years before Google revolutionized personal email products.

Threats

- As can be inferred from the analysis so far, Microsoft's biggest threat is that it's very size which is an asset otherwise is preventing it from being quick and nimble and seize market opportunities by proactively reading market signals.
- Further, Microsoft faces a key challenge from Open Source software, which was a force to reckon with initially seemed to have lost some of its fizz though it is making a comeback again.
- On the commercial front, Microsoft has been exasperated with software piracy especially in Asia where the pirated copies are more than the original products in China and India.
- Finally, Microsoft has to be both weary and wary of potential lawsuits especially in Europe where the regulators are not taking kindly to its monopolistic business practices.

Conclusion

The preceding analysis has made it clear that Microsoft cannot afford to misread emerging trends and changing customer preferences anymore. Instead, it must be in a position where it senses and intuits market moves and prepares to act accordingly. A possible strategic move would be to focus more on the enterprise segment since most other technology companies seem to be focusing exclusively on the personal customer segment. In conclusion, it remains to be seen as to how the recent leadership changes play themselves out with regards to the future strategic moves by the company.

Chapter-VIII

SWOT Analysis of China Mobile

- **Introduction**

China Mobile is a Chinese Telecom major that has been in the news in recent years because of its jaw dropping growth rates as well as its ballooning subscriber base. Once considered as a protected state owned enterprise incapable of efficiency, it has now transformed itself into a domineering company in China with global dreams and ambitions to conquer international markets. As the succeeding SWOT Analysis indicates, the company can leverage on its strengths and work on its weaknesses so that the threats are transformed into opportunities and it continues to be a company to reckon with.

Strengths

- Over the last few decades, China has transformed itself into an economic powerhouse and this is the key strength of China Mobile that was unheard of in Western capitals and for western investors until a decade ago. Indeed, the fact that China Mobile was ranked in the Top 100 Important Brands in the World in 2007 means that it has well and truly arrived in the global arena.
- The company boasts of an incredible number of customers (estimated to be nearly half a Billion) which is a key strength though it must be mentioned that since it is a state owned enterprise and operates in a monopolistic market, these figures are partly due to its domineering presence in the country.
- China mobile is growing at a scorching pace nearing 50% annually which means that in a few years time, it would be way ahead of the global competition by any yardstick.
- Finally, the company has embarked on an international expansion to increase its global footprint and it has been on a merger and acquisition spree especially in Africa, which is touted to be the next emerging frontier.

Weaknesses

- A key weakness of China mobile is that it is not yet ahead of the technology curve though it has the numbers and the volumes to justify its leadership position. This is partly due to the problems that it had in shifting from CDMA to GSM protocol because of the legacy handsets and associated problems and hence, the company was unable to make the transition to the 3G network in a seamless manner.

- Another weakness is that China mobile so far has restricted itself largely to the domestic market. Though we had mentioned about its international expansion, the fact that it is yet to tap into the developed west signals a hesitation and a lack of confidence in taking on global biggies in their backyards.

- Even for the expansion into Africa, China mobile is relying heavily on its partnerships with local players, which means that it is yet to develop an international identity of its own.

Opportunities

- As China continues to grow at a scorching pace, the company can expect a huge jump in its subscriber base though the overheated domestic market might compel it to look outwards for its expansion in the years to come. However, this does not detract from the fact that China mobile is poised to tap into the growing domestic market albeit in a restrained manner unlike the previous years where it was uber aggressive in its strategies.

- As with many other SOEs or State Owned Enterprises in China, the company has recorded annualized profit growth rates in excess of 20%, which has made western investors, look at it with excitement as such profit rates are unheard of in the developed west.

- It can convert its weakness of being unable to transition to 3G technology into an opportunity by tapping into the rural market in China which is still to be explored meaning that China Mobile can start afresh without any legacy issues troubling it. Moreover, as the cities become saturated, it is only natural that China Mobile starts to look to the rural hinterland for future growth.

Threats

- The Chinese telecom sector is still heavily regulated and screened off from international competition, which is a threat as the Chinese government in recent years has been contemplating opening up of the sector to foreign firms. Further, China Mobile also needs to be wary of competition from local firms and domestic players as the industry opens up in the future.

- Another key threat to China Mobile's profitability is that until now it has been playing the "numbers game" wherein it added subscribers mostly in the low price, low value segment, which means that it is a volumes player rather than a premium player. With recent technological breakthroughs like 4G and even 3G, China Mobile faces a threat to its business model and it has to offer higher value added services to stay in the reckoning.

- Its cozy relationship with the Chinese Government is partly because it is a SOE and this might change in the future with the gradual opening up of the economy wherein the government would most likely asses the tradeoff between social dividends and economic payoffs.

Conclusion

As the preceding SWOT Analysis indicates, China Mobile has its task cut out as it begins its international journey and continues its domestic market leadership. As things stand, many western investors are eyeing its stock which is clearly an achievement considering that its IPO (Initial Public Offering) in 1997 hardly attracted interest outside Hong Kong where it started its evolution from a limited player to a market leadership position.

Chapter-IX

SWOT Analysis of Unilever

- **Introduction**

Unilever operates in nearly 190 countries around the world and has been a traditional paragon of excellence and quality in the Fast Moving Consumer Goods sector. The company derives its competitive advantage from its global footprint and its track record of enhancing value for the consumers around the world. Even in the current recessionary environment, it has managed to grow at a respectable pace though as we shall discuss latter, Unilever cannot afford to ignore the emerging threats from a wide range of global, regional, and local players. Apart from this, as the succeeding SWOT Analysis makes it clear, the battle for the emerging markets is likely to escalate into a no holds barred competition with a race to the bottom ensuing between the global giants like Unilever and Proctor and Gamble and a array of local players.

> *Strengths*

- Unilever operates in nearly 190 countries around the world and hence, has a global footprint combined with top of the mind brand recall among consumers worldwide.
- It has a deep and broad portfolio of brands and a diversified product range, which makes it uniquely, positioned to tap into the changing consumer preferences across the world.
- Its Research and Development initiatives are heavily funded and manage to bring to the market innovative and cutting edge products in tune and in line with consumer preferences.
- Unilever has a distinct competitive advantage over its nearest competitor, Proctor and Gamble because of its flexible pricing and expertise in distribution channels that manage to reach the nook and the corner of the globe.
- The company finds its strengths in leveraging the economies of scale arising from its breadth of operations as well as synergies between its many manufacturing facilities, which totaled 270 locations around the world at last count.

- Unilever combines global thinking with local execution, which means that it pursues Glocal strategies that let it win the hearts and minds of consumers who would like to use its products that are globally famous yet retain a distinct local flavor.

Weaknesses

- The biggest weakness that Unilever faces is that it operates in an uber competitive market where the other global giants like P&G and Nestle in addition to a host of local players challenge its dominance at every turn and raise the stakes in the Trillion Dollar FMCG (Fast Moving Consumer Goods) space.
- The other weakness is that its products can easily be replaced with substitutes especially in the emerging markets in Africa and Asia where the rural consumers in the hinterland often use traditional and natural alternatives to the products that Unilever markets.

- *Opportunities*

- With the advent of globalization and the proliferation of global media, consumers in the emerging markets are aspiring to western lifestyles and this means that Unilever has a tremendous opportunity waiting for it as it taps into this large and diversified consumer base that wants to join the league of westerners in taste and preferences for consumer goods.
- Apart from that, capturing the "Newly Affluent Trillion Dollar Consumers" in China and India means that it has a golden opportunity to leverage this huge and growing consumer base, which often tries to imitate and mimic the consumerist preferences of the material west.
- The emergence of the health conscious consumer in the developed world means that Unilever can seize the opportunity to market to this segment with its existing and yet to be launched product range that is specially geared for the health conscious consumer.
- Unilever has a good track record of social and environment responsibility and with the emergence of the ethical chic consumer who like to buy and consume products and brands that are responsibly made and sustainably complete.

- ***Threats***

  ➢ The ongoing global economic crisis has severely dented the profitability of many FMCG companies and Unilever is no exception. With the shrinking of the disposable incomes of the global consumer, they are buying less and insisting on more value for their money or "more bang for the buck". This means that Unilever faces the threat of diminished revenues and increasing costs, which is like a "Double Whammy" to its top-line, and bottom-line.

  ➢ Though we had mentioned that Unilever succeeds and scores over P&G in the CSR or the Corporate Social Responsibility aspect, the increased awareness among the global consumers has turned the harsh glare into each and every strategic move that the company makes. Some practices of the company have been criticized which means that Unilever has to ensure that it sustains and maintains its focus especially when the spotlight is on it.

  ➢ As mentioned earlier, Unilever operates in a market segment where local products and alternatives to its brands proliferate especially in the emerging markets and hence, it faces a threat from smaller and more nimble local upstarts who can provide more value for lesser money without the associated costs that global giants like Unilever incur.

  ➢ The entry of Asian multinationals into the global arena has upped the ante for Unilever and raised the stakes in the global game for dominance in the FMCG market segment. This means that Unilever faces the prospect of having to battle not only the recessionary blues but also emerging threats from this new age and new breed of competition from Asian conglomerates that are beginning to spread their wings internationally.

  ➢ **Conclusion**

Unilever has been in the business of consumer fulfillment for many decades and hence, we are confident that it can tide over the present gloomy conditions in the FMCG segment. Having said that, we conclude the article with a cautionary note of not taking the threat from the Asian FMCG majors lightly as they understand the continent better and at the same time are mastering the intricacies of the global marketplace.

Chapter-X

PESTLE ANALYSIS

▪ Introduction

When we think of airlines, we usually think of luxury and opulence as well as comfort and convenience. However, beneath the veneer, the airlines worldwide are caught in a cycle of higher operating costs, lower profits, and decreasing margins because of the various factors discussed in this article. Though the passengers might not notice these aspects, it is the case that once one scratches the surface and does some research, it is clear that the airline industry is in a mess and only, radical restructuring can help revive its fortunes. The PESTLE methodology is a useful tool to analyze the current state of the airline industry.

PESTLE Analysis of Airlines Industry

➢ *Political*

The political environment in which airlines operate is highly regulated and favors the passengers over the airlines. This is because of the fact that the global aviation industry operates in an environment where passenger safety is paramount and where, the earlier tendencies towards monopolistic behavior by the airlines have made the political establishment weary of the airlines and hence, they have resorted to tighter regulation of the operations of the airlines. Further, the global aviation industry is also characterized by deregulation on the supply side meaning more competition among airlines and regulation on the demand side meaning passengers and fliers are in a position where they can press for more amenities and low prices.

➢ *Economic*

The global airline industry never really recovered from the aftermath of the 911 attacks. Added to this was the prolonged recession in the wake of the dotcom bubble bursting. The other debilitating factor was the fluctuations in the price of oil because of the Second Iraq War and the subsequent spike in oil prices just before The Great Recession of 2008. This last aspect or the ongoing global economic slowdown has meant that the already struggling airlines now have to contend with declining passenger traffic, competition from low cost carriers, high aviation fuel prices, labor demands, and soaring maintenance and operating costs. All these factors have made the airlines loss making and prone to bankruptcies and closure because they can no longer afford to run their operations profitably. Of course, this has also resulted in greater consolidation among the airlines as they seek to leverage the efficiencies from the economies of scale and the synergies from the merger with other airlines.

> ### *Social*

In the recent years, the emergence of the Millennial generation into the consumer class has meant that the social changes of a generation used to entitlement, instant gratification, and more demanding in terms of service has resulted in the airlines having to balance their costs with the increasing demands from this segment. Added to this is the retiring of the Baby Boomer generation that has resulted in the airlines losing a lucrative source of income. Next, the profile of the passengers has changed with more economically minded passengers and less business class passengers who prefer to leverage on the improved communication facilities to conduct meetings remotely instead of flying down to meet their business partners.

> ### *Technological*

Though it is a fact that the airline industry uses technology extensively in its operations, they are limited to the aircraft and the operations of the airlines excluding the ticketing and the distribution aspects. This has prompted many experts to call on the airlines to make use of the advances in technology for the front office and the customer facing functions as well. In other words, the technological changes have to be adapted to include mobile technologies as far as ticketing, distribution, and customer service are concerned. Further, social media has to be leveraged by the airlines to ensure that the boarder social and technological changes do not pass by the airline industry.

> *Legal*

In recent years, the number of lawsuits against airlines from both customers as well as workers has gone up. Further, the regulators are being stricter with the airlines, which mean that they are now increasingly wary of their strategies, and actualizing their strategies only after they are fully convinced that they are not violating any laws. The "double whammy" of increased regulation and more expensive lawsuits apart from the legal system becoming intolerant of delays, safety issues, and other aspects has only served to heighten the fears among the airlines as each and every move of theirs is being scrutinized.

> *Environmental*

With climate change entering the social consciousness, passengers are now counting their carbon footprint with the result that they are now more environmentally conscious. This has resulted in the airlines being forced to adopt "green flying" and be more responsive to the concerns of the environmentalists. Further, the social responsibility initiatives are becoming more pronounced and more under scrutiny as consumers and activists turn a critical eye towards the airlines and their corporate social responsibility.

> **Conclusion: The Airline Death Spiral**

The discussion so far leads to the conclusion that the global airline industry is now in a phase where the "Airline Death Spiral" has taken over. This has resulted in a wave of bankruptcies and closure of airlines worldwide. Further, the regulators are not lenient with airlines when they ask for more time or ask for less strict rules and regulations. Apart from this, the demanding fliers and competition from low cost airlines means that full service airlines can no longer compete on price or volume. Finally, the increased costs of doing business have dented the profitability and the viability of the global airline industry.

Chapter-XI

PESTLE Analysis of Starbucks

- ## Introduction

The macroeconomic environment that Starbucks operates in is characterized by the ongoing global economic recession, which has dented the purchasing power of the consumers. However, market research done in the last few months has indicated that consumers have not cut down on their coffee consumption and instead, are shifting to lower priced options. This means that Starbucks can still leverage the buying power of the consumers in a manner that would give it a significant advantage over its rivals by offering cheaper alternatives. Apart from this, Starbucks has already made some moves to jump on the emerging mobile computing revolution by tying up with Apple to introduce discounted coupons in the apps used in the iPhones. Further, this exercise has also been accompanied by co-branding and cross selling which means, that Starbucks is well placed and poised to reap the benefits of the Smartphone revolution. Having said that, it must be noted that consumers in the United States are increasingly turning "Ethical Chic" which means that the products they buy and the brands they consume need to prove that they are following social and environmental norms in their manufacture. This is the key challenge that Starbucks faces as it confronts the emerging challenges of the new era of consumer awareness and the galloping Smartphone revolution.

- ## *Political*

- ➢ The key political imperative that Starbucks faces is the concerns over sourcing of its raw materials that has attracted the attention of the politicians in the West and in the countries from where it sources its raw materials. This is the reason why Starbucks is keen on adhering to social and environmental norms and to follow sourcing strategies that are appropriate and in conformance to the "Fair Trade" practices that have been agreed upon by global corporations and the governments of the developing and the developed countries.

- ➢ The other political imperative that Starbucks faces is the need to adhere to the laws and regulations in the countries from where it sources its raw materials. This has been necessitated because of activism and increased political awareness in the developing countries, which form the basis for Starbucks' sourcing strategies.

➢ The third political imperative, which Starbucks faces, is the regulatory pressures within its home market in the United States because of greater scrutiny of the business processes that multinationals based in the US are now subject to.

➢ *Economic*

▪ The foremost external economic driver for Starbucks is the ongoing global economic recession, which as explained in the introduction has dented the profitability of many companies.

▪ However, studies have shown that consumers instead of cutting down on their coffee consumption are shifting to lower priced alternatives which is an opportunity for Starbucks.

▪ Of course, the company still has to contend with rising operational and labor costs as the inflationary macroeconomic environment coupled with the falling profitability is squeezing the company from both ends of the spectrum.

➢ *Socio-Cultural*

▪ Though Starbucks can offer cheaper alternatives as mentioned previously, it has to do so without sacrificing the quality and this is the key socio cultural challenge that the company faces as it expands its consumer base to include the consumers from the lower and the middle tiers of the income pyramid.

▪ Apart from this, the "green" and the "ethical chic" consumers who fret about the social and environmental costs of the brands they consumer means that Starbucks has to be cognizant of this trend.

▪ Third, the retiring baby boomer generation means that spending by the older consumers is likely to taper off and hence, Starbucks would have to lookout for tapping the Gen X and the Millennials as part of its strategy.

- ➤ *Technological*

- ➤ Starbucks is well poised to reap the benefits of the emerging mobile wave and as it has tied up with Apple to introduce app based discount coupons, it can expect to ride the mobile wave with ease.
- ➤ The company has already introduced Wi-Fi capabilities in its outlets so that consumers can surf the web and do their work while sipping coffee. This is indeed an added value to the Starbucks brand and something, which enhances the consumer experience.
- ➤ It can also introduce mobile payments and this is something that it is already testing out in pilot locations in the United States.

- ➤ *Legal*

- Starbucks has to ensure that it does not run afoul of the laws and regulations in the countries from which it sources its raw materials as well as the home markets in the United States.

- ➤ *Environmental*

- There have been several concerns about the business practices of Starbucks from the activists, international advocacy groups, and from the consumers themselves. Therefore, Starbucks has to take into account these concerns if it has to continue holding on to the trust it enjoys with its consumers.

- ➤ **Conclusion**

The preceding analysis proves the point that Starbucks is operating in a relatively stable external environment. The main reason for this is the fact that it operates in the Food and Beverages space which means that despite the recession, consumers cut down on the consumption to a certain extent and not completely. Therefore, the task before Starbucks is to lower costs and increase the value so that it retains its consumer base and attracts consumer loyalty.

Chapter-XII
PESTLE Analysis of Samsung

- ## Introduction

Samsung is a global conglomerate that operates in the "White Goods" market or the market for consumer appliances and gadgets. The company that is a South Korean family owned business has global aspirations and as the recent expansion into newer markets has shown, Samsung is not content with operating in some markets in the world but instead, wants to cover as many countries as possible. Therefore, the focus of this article is on the external environmental drivers of Samsung's strategy.

> ### *Political*

In most of the markets where Samsung operates, the political environment is conducive to its operations and though there are minor irritants in some of the foreign markets like India, overall Samsung can be said to be operating in markets where the political factors are benign. However, in recent months, it has faced significant political headwinds in its home country of South Korea because of the country's tensions with North Korea wherein the company has had to take into account not only the political instability but also the threat of war breaking out in the Korean Peninsula. Apart from this, Samsung faces political pressures in many African and Latin American countries where the political environment is unstable and prone to frequent changes in the governing structures. Of course, this is not yet a major cause for worry as the company has more or less factored the political instability into its strategic calculations.

> ### *Economic*

This dimension is especially critical for Samsung, as the opening up of many markets in the developing world has meant that the company can expand its global footprint. However, this dimension is also a worry since the ongoing global economic crisis has severely dented the purchasing power of consumers in many developed markets forcing Samsung to seek profitable ventures in the emerging markets. The key point to note here is that the macroeconomic environment in which Samsung operates globally is beset with uncertainty and volatility leading to the company having had to reorient its strategies accordingly. The saving grace for the company is that it has adjusted rather well to the tapering off of the consumer disposable incomes in the developed world by expanding into the emerging and the developing markets. Indeed, this is the reason Samsung has begun an aggressive push into the emerging markets in the hope of making up for lost business from the developed world.

> ### *Socio-Cultural*

Samsung is primarily a South Korean Chaebol or a family owned multinational. This means that despite its global footprint it still operates from the core as a Korean company. Therefore, there are several aspects to its global operations some of which include adapting itself to the local conditions. In other words, Samsung being a Global company has had to act locally meaning that it has had to adopt a Glocal strategy in many emerging markets. Apart from this, Samsung has had to tailor its products to the fast changing consumer preferences in the various markets where it operates. The key point to note here is that Samsung operates in a market niche that is strongly influenced by the lifestyle preferences of consumers and given the fact that socio cultural factors are different in each country; it has had to reorient itself in each market accordingly.

> ### *Technological*

Samsung can be considered as being among the world's leading innovative companies. This means that the company is at an advantage as far as harnessing the power of technology and driving innovation for sustainable business advantage is concerned. This has translated into an obsessive mission by the company to be ahead of the technological and innovation curve and a vision to dominate its rivals and competitors as far being the first to reach the market with its latest products is concerned. however, as we shall discuss later, this has also resulted in the company cutting corners with its imitation of the legendary Apple's product design and this has brought legal and regulatory scrutiny and troubles for the company. There is a lesson here for other technology driven companies from Samsung's experiences and it is that no matter how fast you are to reach the consumer in this age of Big Bang Disruption, doing the basics right is still the key to success.

➢ *Legal*

As mentioned in the last section, Samsung has had to face heavy penalties for its alleged imitation of the Apple's iPad and iPhone and this has led to the company taking a beating as far as public perceptions and consumer approval of its strategies are concerned. It remains to be seen as to how the company would wriggle out of the legal maze that it finds itself in the developed markets because of the various lawsuits.

➢ *Environmental*

With the rise of the ethical consumer who wants his or her brands to source and make the products in a socially and environmentally responsible manner, Samsung has to be aware of the need to make its products to satiate the ethical chic consumer. This means that it has to ensure that it does not compromise on the working conditions or the wages it pays to its labor who are engaged in making the final product.

➢ Conclusion

The preceding analysis clearly indicates that Samsung has its task cut out for itself as it navigates the treacherous global consumer market landmine. Indeed, as the company prepares to expand its global footprint, the stakes could not have been higher in a recessionary era and an uber competitive technological market landscape.

stamford business reviews

Chapter-XIII

Porter's Five Forces Analysis of Airlines Industry in the USA

- ## Introduction

Porter's Five Forces analysis is a useful methodology and a tool to analyze the external environment in which any industry operates. The key aspect about using Porter's Five Forces for the airline industry in the United States is that the airline industry has been buffeted by strong headwinds from a host of external factors that include declining passenger traffic, increasing operating expenses, high fuel prices, and greater landing and maintenance costs, apart from intense competition from low cost carriers that has led to a cutthroat price war which has led the industry severely affected. Indeed, it can be said that the airline industry globally is in a "death spiral" and more so in the United States where several prominent carriers were either forced into bankruptcy or had to merge with other airlines just to stay afloat.

- ## Supplier Power

The power of suppliers in the airline industry is immense because of the fact that the three inputs that airlines have in terms of fuel, aircraft, and labor are all affected by the external environment. For instance, the price of aviation fuel is subject to the fluctuations in the global market for oil, which can gyrate wildly because of geopolitical and other factors. Similarly, labor is subject to the power of the unions who often bargain and get unreasonable and costly concessions from the airlines. Third, the airline industry needs aircraft either on outright sale or wet lease basis which means that the airlines have to depend on the two biggies, Airbus, and Boeing for their aircraft needs. This is the reason the power of the suppliers in terms of the three inputs needed for them is categorized as high according to the Porter's Five Forces framework.

- ## Buyer Power

With the proliferation of online ticketing and distribution systems, fliers no longer have to be at the mercy of the agents and the intermediaries as well the airlines themselves for their ticketing needs. Apart from, the entry of low cost carriers and the resultant price wars has greatly benefited the fliers. Moreover, the tight regulation on the demand side of the airline industry meaning that passengers and fliers have been protected by the regulators means that the balance of power is tipped in their favor. All these factors make the airline industry cede power to the consumers and hence, the power of buyers is moderate to high as per Porter's Five Forces methodology. Apart from this, the buyers can engage in "price discovery" meaning that price fluctuations do not deter them as they have multiple channels through which they can book their tickets.

- **Entry and Exit Barriers**

The airline industry needs huge capital investment to enter and even when airlines have to exit the sector, they need to write down and absorb many losses. This means that the entry and exit barriers are high for the airline industry. As entry into the airline industry needs a high infusion of capital, not everybody can enter the industry, which in addition, needs sophisticated knowledge and expertise on part of the players, which is a deterrent. The exit barriers are also subject to regulation as regulators in the United States do not let airlines exit the industry unless they are satisfied that there is a genuine business reason for the same. Moreover, the airline industry leverages the efficiencies and the synergies from the economies of scale and hence, the entry barriers are high. Therefore, applying Porter's Five Forces framework, we find that the airlines pose significant entry and exit barriers, which means that the impact of this dimension is quite high.

- **Threat of Substitutes and Complementarities**

The airline industry in the United States is not at threat from substitutes and complementarities as unlike in the developing world, consumers do not necessarily take the train or the bus for journeys. What this means is that flying is a natural phenomenon for the consumers and hence, the substitutes in terms of the train and bus is minimal in its impact. Of course, many Americans motor down (use their cars for longer travel as well) which means that there is the threat of this substitute. As for complementarities, the provision of services like free Wi-Fi, a la carte meals, and passenger amenities offered by the full service airlines does not really translate into more passengers as in the recent past; fliers have been induced more by lower fares than these aspects.

- **Intensity of Competitive Rivalry**

As mentioned in the introduction, the airline industry in the United States is extremely competitive because of a number of reasons which include entry of low cost carriers, the tight regulation of the industry wherein safety become paramount leading to high operating expenses, and the fact that the airlines operate according to a business model that is a bit outdated especially in times of rapid turnover and churn in the industry. Apart from anything else, the airline industry is regulated on the supply side more than the demand side, which means that instead of the airlines being free to choose which markets to operate and which segments to target, it is the fliers who get to be pampered by the regulators. This is the reason why low cost carriers have literally grounded the full service airlines and when combined with the intense competition that was always the case in the United States, the result is that the sector is one of the most competitive in the country.

Chapter-XIV

Porter's Five Forces Analysis of Samsung

- ## Introduction

Porter's Five Forces methodology is used in this article to analyze the business strategies of white goods makers like Samsung. This tool is a handy method to assess how each of the market drivers impact the companies like Samsung and then based on the analysis, suitable business strategies can be devised. Further, companies like Samsung are known to study the markets they want to approach thoroughly and deeply before they make a move and it is in this perspective that this analysis is undertaken.

- ## Industry Rivalry

This element is especially significant for Samsung as the other White Goods multinationals like LG, Nokia, and Motorola not to mention Apple are engaged in fierce competitive rivalry. Indeed, Samsung cannot take its position in the market for granted as all these and other domestic white goods players operate in a market where margins are tight and the competition is intense. Apart from this, Samsung faces the equivalent of the "Cola Wars" (the legendary fight for dominance between Coke and Pepsi) in emerging markets like India where Samsung has to contend and compete with a multitude of players domestic and global. This has made the impact of this dimension especially strong for Samsung.

- ## Barriers to Entry and Exit

The White Goods industry is characterized by high barriers to entry and low barriers to exit especially where global conglomerates like Samsung are concerned. Indeed, it is often very difficult to enter emerging markets because a host of factors have to be taken into consideration such as setting up the distribution network and the supply chain. However, global conglomerates can exit the emerging markets easily as all it takes is to handover and sell the business to a domestic or a foreign player in the case of declining or falling sales. This means that Samsung has entered many emerging markets through a step-by-step approach and has also exited the markets that have been found to be unprofitable. This is the reason why white goods multinationals like Samsung often do their due diligence before entering emerging markets.

- **Power of Buyers**

The power of buyers for white goods makers like Samsung is somewhat of a mixed bag where though the buyers have a multitude of options to choose from and at the same time have to stick with the product since they cannot just dump the product, as it is a high value item. Further, the buyers would have to necessarily approach the companies for after sales service and for spare parts. Of course, this does not mean that the buyers are at the mercy of the companies. Far from that, they do have power over the companies, as most emerging market consumers are known to be finicky when deciding on the product to buy and explore all the options before reaching a decision. This means that both the buyers and the companies need each other just like the suppliers and the companies, as we shall discuss next.

- **Power of Suppliers**

In many markets in which Samsung operates, there are many suppliers who are willing to offer their services at a discount since the ancillary sectors are very deep. However, this does not mean that the companies can exert undue force over the suppliers as once the supply chain is established; it takes a lot to undo it and build a new supply chain afresh. This is the reason why white goods makers like Samsung invariably study the markets before setting up shop and also take the help of consultancies in arriving at their decision.

- **Threat of Substitutes**

This element is indeed high as the markets for white goods are flooded with many substitutes and given the fact that consumer durables are often longer term purchases, companies like Samsung have to be careful in deciding on the appropriate marketing strategy. This is also the reason why many multinationals like Samsung often adopt differential pricing so as to attract consumers from across the income pyramid to wean them away from cheaper substitutes. Further, this element also means that many emerging market consumers are yet to deepen their dependence on white goods and instead, prefer to the traditional forms of housework wherein they rely less on gadgets and appliances. However, this is rapidly changing as more women enter the workforce in these markets making it necessary for them to use gadgets and appliances.

- **Stakeholders**

This is an added element for analysis as the increasing concern over social and environmentally conscious business practices means that companies like Samsung have to be careful in how they do business as well as project themselves to the consumers. For instance, white goods makers are known to decide after due deliberation on everything from choosing their brand ambassadors to publicizing their CSR (Corporate Social Responsibility) initiatives.

- **Conclusion**

As the diagram above indicates the relative strengths and the weaknesses of each element, we can now conclude this analysis with the theme that as the global economy integrates and more emerging markets open up, companies like Samsung are at an advantage because they have already established themselves in many markets. However, it must also be noted that each market is unique and hence, Samsung must not adopt a one size fits all strategy and instead, must approach each market differently. In conclusion, Samsung can take pride from the fact that being an Asian conglomerate, it has managed to break into and hold its own against many western multinationals that have been in this business for decades.

Chapter-XV

Porter's Five Forces Analysis of Virgin Atlantic

- **Introduction**

To introduce the article, it would suffice to say that each of the five forces that are discussed subsequently differ in their impact on Virgin Atlantic as the dynamics underlying them vary and the strategy employed by the airline is subject to the fluid and the changing external environment. Virgin Atlantic is a pioneer in the low cost business model though in recent years, many of its competitors have successfully incorporated its strategies in their operations.

Entry and Exit Barriers

The entry and the exit barriers for the aviation industry are quite high as can be seen from the fact that it takes a lot of capital to enter the sector. Further, airlines cannot exit the sector when they choose as the regulators often insist that they fulfill their contractual obligations towards their stakeholders in case they want to exit the venture. Apart from this, the airline industry is characterized by tight regulation and many rules, which means that the regulators have to be satisfied about the safety aspect in addition to the airworthiness and the financial stability of the carriers. This means that the entry barriers are formidable and hence, Virgin Atlantic faces an external environment that is relatively tough for newer entrants to entrench themselves. Having said that, it must be remembered that once a carrier enters the industry, the situation is different as it can then engage in all out price wars and a race to the bottom.

Industry Rivalry

It is a known fact that the airline industry is saturated with more and more carriers entering the sector in search of profits. Though it is a separate matter that most airlines do not manage to make profits consistently, this has not deterred the carriers from setting shop and entering the industry. Therefore, it can be said that the industry rivalry is quite high and something that affects Virgin Atlantic very much. Further, as far as the global aviation industry is concerned, there is a race to the bottom as ever-increasing carriers vie for a shrinking passenger pie leading to fare wars and cutthroat competition. Apart from this, the rivalry between airlines is leading to more consolidation as the mantra of bigger is better and lack of profitability is driving the airlines towards mega mergers.

Power of Suppliers

The suppliers for carriers like Virgin Atlantic are the aircraft makers like Boeing and Airbus in addition to the aviation fuel companies and the ground support and handling vendors. Further, the suppliers also include those who make spare parts to the airlines. Considering the fact that the airline industry is characterized by the presence of a few carriers and many suppliers vying for business, it comes as no surprise that the power of the suppliers is low and the airlines have the upper hand in their interactions with the suppliers. Further, even in cases such as the supply of jet fuel, the carriers like Virgin Atlantic have a distinct advantage, as this fuel is expensive and a premium product meaning that there are not too many buyers for it making Virgin Atlantic a favored customer for the aviation fuel companies.

Power of Buyers

If there is one force that has the maximum amount of impact on Virgin Atlantic, it is the power of buyers because the airline industry is essentially a buyers' market because of a plethora of choices, intense fare wars, and the ever looming threat of low cost carriers eating into the market share of established rivals. Of course, Virgin Atlantic is itself a low cost carrier though the fact that in recent years, many airlines have successfully imitated its business model means that they are taking away fliers from it. Further, with regulators choosing to lean on the side of the buyers rather than the airlines, Virgin Atlantic has to kowtow to the fliers and defer to them as otherwise it would lose out on market share. Apart from this, the increase in the distribution channels through which fliers can buy tickets and the removal of the intermediary layer with the proliferation of online booking direct from the airlines means that the buyers are spoilt for choice.

Threat of Substitutes

People in the West most often travel by air and hence, the threat of substitutes is not that high for Virgin Atlantic. Having said that, it must be remembered that due to the ongoing recession, many business fliers who hitherto used to fly are now considering other options like Teleconferencing, virtual meetings, and such things to reduce the need to fly down to the customer and the partner locations for business meetings. Apart from this, another noticeable trend in recent years has been the paring down of leisure travel and substituting it with cheaper options like budget cruises and slow tourism that entail less dependency on air travel.

Conclusion

The preceding discussion has highlighted the impact of each of the five forces as detailed in the Porters framework on Virgin Atlantic. The clear implications that one can draw from this is that Virgin Atlantic faces a competitive and a challenging external environment that directly affects its operations as it has to innovate and be lean and mean in its operational capacities and capabilities if it has to survive the onslaught of competition. Before concluding this article, it would be pertinent to point that the global airline industry is in a death spiral and hence, Virgin Atlantic has to be ahead of the curve if it has to remain profitable.

Chapter-XVI

Porters Five Forces Analysis of China Mobile

▪ Introduction

China Mobile operates in a monopoly like market in the domestic Chinese telecom sector and hence, the application of the five forces model reveals that it need not yet worry about the external environment, which is protected and heavily regulated. Having said that, as the succeeding discussion makes it clear, it cannot take its current comfort zone for granted, and as the recent strategic moves made by it reveal, it indeed taking steps to ensure that it continues to thrive and prosper even when the Chinese Telecom market is thrown open to foreign competition. However, its status as a SOE or a State Owned Enterprise guarantees it a lead over competitors even in this scenario, as the Chinese government is known to handhold its SOEs even in the face of competition.

Industry Rivalry

As China Mobile operates in a heavily regulated market where the government limits competition, the power of this element is not high. Indeed, it can be said that this element exerts the lowest force, as there are very few domestic or international competitors for China Mobile. Further, the fact that China Mobile is a monopoly player coupled with the large market share it has means that it faces little or no competition from existing or as we shall discuss, new players. Finally, the large industry size with a sizzling growth rate in the volumes of subscribers means that China Mobile does not have to worry too much about Industry Rivalry. However, this is set to change in the future because of the gradual opening up of the Chinese market to foreign firms even in telephony, which is enough for China Mobile to take it seriously. As has been mentioned elsewhere, many of the future trends point to China Mobile having to discard its legacy business model and indeed, current evidence suggests that it is in the process of doing so.

Entry and Exit Barriers

The Telecom sector anywhere in the world has high sunk costs, which means that prospective firms seeking to enter the market have to invest a lot of capital. This is further exacerbated in the Chinese market where the need of a strong distribution network given the size of the country coupled with the lack of advanced technology available to newer players means that this force is medium to low in its strength. Apart from this, the Chinese market as mentioned earlier is tightly regulated with a maze of rules and regulations that govern the market making it difficult for smaller and lesser-known players to enter the market. Therefore, China Mobile has very few reasons to worry about the threat of new players though this seems likely to change in the future with the government deciding to open up the Chinese telecom sector to international competition.

Power of Suppliers

The power of suppliers is virtually nonexistent as there is a single technology standard and given the lack of technological sophistication of the Chinese telecom market, suppliers cannot exert the power of technology on China Mobile. Moreover, as the market is tightly regulated, the suppliers (many of them government owned SOEs or State Owned Enterprises) have no choice but to do business with China Mobile. Of course, this works the other around as well since China Mobile has to rely on the few suppliers for its needs though the government plays the mediating role to ensure that neither side holds the other to ransom.

Power of Buyers

As with the other forces, the power of buyers is limited because of the presence of very few players in the Chinese Telecom sector. Coupled with the fact that there is low price sensitivity and low dependency on customization, China Mobile has a near stranglehold on the market as can be seen from the way it has acquired a large customer base within the span of a decade. This large customer base also gives China Mobile the power to set prices though the government intervenes now and then. Further, because of the premium that the Chinese place on owning a mobile handset and a connection, they are willing to endure the waiting period and the necessary adjustments, which mean that China Mobile has the free run of the market.

Threat of Substitutes

Given the fact that China is still a primarily agrarian country where the hinterland continues to languish though the cities are world class, the substitutes to mobile telephony are very few. With China being like other emerging markets where the transition from postal communication to telephony did not go through the landline phase and instead, leapfrogged into the mobile phase, China Mobile need not bother about landline substitution though the gradual adoption of the internet has made it wary of potential substitutes from internet telephony. Apart from this, China Mobile is also actively expanding into the internet based communications so that it retains its market share in the online realm as well.

Conclusion

The preceding analysis has revealed the theme that China Mobile needs to start preparing for the future as soon as possible because of the trends like allowing competition, upgrading technology, opening up to foreign firms, and most importantly, the advent of internet telephony that threatens the cozy market leadership, which China Mobile has. In conclusion, the future seems to be arriving faster than expected for China Mobile and hence, it is the case that it needs to prepare for the future as though it has arrived yesterday.

Author

Prof.Lavakush Singh

M.Com(Accounting & Taxation) M.Com(Cost & Works Accounting), M.Com(BusinessAdministration),MA(Economics),MBA(Finance) ,MA(Sociology),UGC(NET),in Commerce, PhD(Business Administration)

Prof. Lavakush Singh is an Assistant Professor in Abeda Inamdar Senior College, Pune University. Prior to joining this college, he has been teaching in a management Institute affiliated to university of Pune.He received his graduation in commerce from Kanpur University & Master degree from university of Pune. During his intensive teaching spanning a decade, he taught subjects on different arena, namely, Principles of Management, Cost Accounting, Mercantile law, Managerial Economics, Strategic Management & Research Methodology. His research focuses on Public Private Participation in Infrastructure Sector, FDI in Insurance Sector, BRICS Nations & their contributions, New Companies Act 2013 &Demonetisation & its effect on various sectors of Indian Economy. He has authored 6 books of different domains of business, Commerce & Economy, namely, Marketing Management :An Asian Perspective , Elements of marketing Management, Essentials of Strategic Management , Cases in Strategic Management, handbook of Strategic Management , Business economics , Managerial Economics. Along with this, He has published over one 20 National and 5international research papers in numerous journals and international conference proceedings. He was given letter of appreciation by former Deputy Chairman : Planning Chairman India for his paper on expenditure tax in India .Prof. Lavakush Singh has also held various assignments namely Placement Coordinator, Centre Head: PAI Career Academy and commanded 1 Maratha Signal Company of Army as an Associate NCC Officer .He received Certification on Multivariate Analysis & Academic Leadership using SPSS & Minitab.

21222756R00035

Printed in Great Britain
by Amazon